AMERICA DEBATES™

AMERICA DEBATES UNITED STATES POLICY ON IMMIGRATION

Renee Ambrosek

rosen publishing's
rosen central®

New York

Published in 2008 by The Rosen Publishing Group, Inc.
29 East 21st Street, New York, NY 10010

First Edition

Library of Congress Cataloging-in-Publication Data

Ambrosek, Renee.
America debates United States policy on immigration/Renee Ambrosek.
    p. cm.—(America debates)
Includes bibliographical references and index.
ISBN-13: 978-1-4042-1924-3
ISBN-10: 1-4042-1924-2
1. United States—Emigration and immigration—Government policy.
2. United States—Emigration and immigration. 3. Immigrants—United States. I. Title.
JV6483.A439 2007
325.73—dc22

                                                    2006101215

Manufactured in the United States of America

On the cover: *(Left)* A member of the Minuteman Civil Defense Corps patrols the U.S.-Mexico border on April 8, 2006. *(Right)* Protesters rally in the streets of Boston for justice for all immigrants on April 10, 2006.

CONTENTS

Introduction

If the Statue of Liberty could talk, what do you think she would say? What does the Statue of Liberty represent to you? In 1883, shortly before the Statue of Liberty was erected in New York Harbor, an American poet named Emma Lazarus heard about the plans for the giant lady and wrote a poem entitled "The New Colossus." In her poem, Lazarus wrote the words that she imagined the Statue of Liberty would say to the people of the world. Four lines of her poem have become particularly famous:

> Give me your tired, your poor,
> Your huddled masses yearning to breathe free,

Introduction

> The wretched refuse of your teeming shore.
> Send these, the homeless, tempest-tost to me.

Lazarus had hoped that her poem would inspire people to donate money to help fund the building of the statue's base, and indeed it did; in fact, her poem became such an instant classic that after the statue was completed, a copy of the poem was inscribed on the base.

"The New Colossus" helped to permanently link the Statue of Liberty to the concept of immigration in the United States. This association was reinforced even more after Ellis Island, the famous immigration processing station, opened up near the Statue of Liberty in 1892. Often, the statue was the first thing that immigrants saw in America after making the hard trip by ship during the late 1800s to mid-1900s.

But think more carefully about the words of Emma Lazarus's famous poem. If you wanted to build a new country and make it prosperous, what kind of people would you want to come and live there? Would you want the most energetic and successful people from other countries, or the "tired and poor"? How many people would you allow in? Just a few, so that your country could absorb them easily, or would you want "huddled masses"? The best and the brightest, or the "wretched refuse"? Would you want those who choose to move because they believe in the ideals and principles that your country was founded on, or those who come because they're "homeless and tempest-tost" and have no other place to go?

When Emma Lazarus wrote "The New Colossus," she was only considering one perspective. She believed strongly that the

5

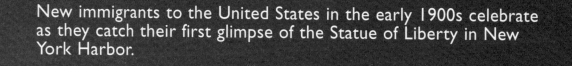

New immigrants to the United States in the early 1900s celebrate as they catch their first glimpse of the Statue of Liberty in New York Harbor.

United States had a responsibility and obligation to be a shelter and a refuge for immigrants. However, her poem highlights some of the problems that Americans have with the issue of immigration. Who should be allowed to come live in America? What kind of people? How many? Further, what rules should be applied to these people when they arrive here? And who gets to decide on those rules? These are questions that Americans have been struggling with since the founding of the country— questions that are still debated within the issue of U.S. immigration policy.

Chapter 1

What Is Immigration?

In order to understand the current debates about U.S. immigration policy, it helps to have a little background on the topic in general. Immigration is as old as humanity itself; people have always moved from one place to another in order to find better resources or to escape threats from natural disasters or hostile neighbors. However, mass immigration of people from one area to another as we know it today was not really possible until relatively recently, when advances in transportation and industrialization made movement easier and more appealing for the average citizen. Every year, as travel and international communication become easier, the rate of global immigration rises.

PUSH AND PULL

When scholars talk about immigration and the reasons that people move, they use the terms "push factors" and "pull factors." Push factors are the things that cause people to decide to emigrate—the negative aspects of a person's home country that make him or her want to leave. For example, a war or famine are two push factors that might make someone decide that life would be better in a new country. Pull factors are the incentives an immigrant sees in a new country that make him or her choose to immigrate there. Lax immigration laws or a strong economy with a lot of job opportunities might be considered pull factors.

However, most of the push and pull factors behind immigration throughout the world are based in economics. Too few job opportunities or an unstable economy can push people to leave an area and look for ways to provide for themselves and their families in a new place. Obviously, the countries with the most potential to provide jobs and economic security for an immigrant will usually be the countries with the strongest pull factor. This is one of the reasons that America is such a popular choice for immigration. By global standards, it has a very strong economy with many job opportunities.

LEGAL AND ILLEGAL IMMIGRATION

Like most countries in the world, the United States requires a prospective immigrant to register with the government and to declare his desire to immigrate when he arrives in the country. If an immigrant properly registers, follows the rules regarding

At a citizenship center in San Jose, California, over 1,700 immigrants recite the Pledge of Allegiance together as they are legally sworn in as naturalized citizens of the United States.

immigration, and is admitted into the United States, he or she is known as a legal immigrant.

A legal immigrant may choose to eventually become a citizen of the United States. Obtaining legal citizenship allows an immigrant to have most of the same legal rights that a natural-born citizen would be entitled to, such as the right to vote and the right to collect benefits such as Social Security. An immigrant who successfully goes through this process becomes known as a naturalized citizen.

However, not everyone who moves to the United States is given permission to stay as a legal immigrant. For that reason, some immigrants enter the country without registering with the government, for fear that they will be denied permission to stay. Others register and are allowed to stay, but then they stop following the rules that they were supposed to follow in order to remain a legal immigrant. People that fall into these categories are known as illegal immigrants.

THE NATURALIZATION PROCESS IN THE UNITED STATES

The road to citizenship in the United States involves the following:

- An immigrant has to have been living and working legally in the United States for at least five years with no legal problems during residency to submit an application for citizenship.
- The application costs nearly $300 to file and requires that the immigrant be fingerprinted, photographed, and interviewed. At the interview, the immigrant is asked to bring several different documents that verify the details of employment, family situation, and residency for the last five years.
- If the applicant passes the screening interview, he or she is asked to take a test on United States history and civics, as well as an English language proficiency test. If the applicant passes these tests, he or she is scheduled for a date to take the oath of citizenship.
- Following the oath of citizenship, the applicant is given a certificate legally proclaiming him or her to be a naturalized citizen.

A woman immigrates to America through Ellis Island with her three children in 1905, during the Great Period of Immigration.

A NATION OF IMMIGRANTS

The United States is often called a nation of immigrants because if you trace every American's ancestry back far enough, you'll find that there really is no such thing as a "pure-bred" American. Everyone in the United States is descended from an immigrant somewhere in his or her family tree. Even the earliest inhabitants of the country, the Native Americans, are believed to have been immigrants, originally coming to this land from Siberia sometime between 30000 and 13000 BC.

Most Americans' immigration experiences happened much more recently, of course. The most famous era of immigration in America occurred between the middle of the 1800s and the beginning of the 1900s. This era is known as the Great Period of Immigration, and during this period, more than thirty million immigrants came to the United States, most of them from

Europe. Famine, overcrowding, and political instability in several European countries were the major push factors for this immigration wave, and America was regarded as a land of limitless opportunity.

However, even though large numbers of immigrants were arriving, it did not always mean that they were welcomed warmly. The rapid increase in new immigrants created slums in many major American cities, as immigrants struggled to establish themselves financially in the new country. Many anti-immigrant groups were created across the country, and anti-immigrant prejudice and discrimination was rampant. Immigrants did not have an easy life in the United States, but many felt that despite these hardships, living the American dream was worth the battle.

IMMIGRATION TODAY

Today, the United States is experiencing another wave of immigration, as more and more people from around the world once again decide that despite the hardships involved with emigrating, life in America is worth the battle. However, Europeans no longer make up the largest group of foreigners wishing to move to America.

After the Great Period of Immigration at the turn of the last century, the government passed laws that set aside immigration quotas for each country. These quotas limited the number of people that could come in from any given country, and once the quota from that country was met, no more immigrants were given legal entry from that country until the next year. Under

A man carries a box of tortillas in the predominantly Hispanic "Little Village" neighborhood in Chicago. The end of the quota system raised the Hispanic population in many U.S. neighborhoods.

this quota system, it was easier to immigrate to the United States if you were coming from a European country, since the countries of Europe had higher quota limits.

However, because many people believed that this system was racist, it was done away with in 1965 when Congress passed a new immigration act. The end of the quota system not only meant that more people could emigrate from non-European countries, but it also meant that a greater concentration of people from the same country could be admitted. The Immigration Act

THE KNOW-NOTHING PARTY

Prejudice against immigrants is nothing new in America. In fact, for a time in U.S. history there was an entire political party based on prejudice against immigrants. The Know-Nothing Party originated in New York in the early 1840s and became a legitimate national political party in 1845. Their name came from the fact that many people were secretly members of the party, and when asked about their party involvement, they were instructed to reply "I know nothing." The Know-Nothings gained mainstream popularity after the Irish Potato Famine caused huge numbers of Irish-Catholic immigrants to come to America. The flood of Catholic immigrants alarmed the predominantly Protestant population of the United States, and the Know-Nothings ran a political platform that advocated restricting Irish immigrants to certain slum neighborhoods and low-wage jobs. The party was short-lived, and most members of the group were absorbed into the Republican Party by 1857. However, during the ten years that they were active, they were responsible for organized racist attacks against Irish-Catholic immigrants, attacks that sometimes became violent. The popular 2002 Leonardo DiCaprio movie *Gangs of New York* is based on the struggles between Irish-Catholic immigrants and members of the Know-Nothing Party.

of 1965 changed more than the quota system, though. It also introduced the "family reunification" policy, which gave favoritism to applicants who already had family members in the United States.

Without a quota limiting the number of immigrants from one country, and because many immigrants from Mexico also already had family members living in the United States, the Immigration Act of 1965 was a direct benefit to Mexican immigrants. Accordingly, the number of immigrants from Mexico began to rise sharply. Currently, people from Latin America are the largest group of immigrants to the United States, with people from different countries on the continent of Asia being the second largest group.

The Immigration Act of 1965 had a big effect on how people around the world viewed the United States as well. When U.S. immigration policy favored Europe, many people from non-European countries thought that immigrating to America from their country was too hard, since there were so many people vying for just a few immigration slots. Now that the quota system is gone, the dream of immigrating to the United States from a non-European country seems more possible to many people. Since the Immigration Act of 1965, the number of immigrants that apply to come to the United States has gone up each year.

Chapter 2

The Economic Debate

Currently, the United States takes in approximately one million immigrants per year, which is more immigrants than all of the other countries in the world combined. In addition, it is estimated that as many as 500,000 illegal immigrants come into the United States per year.

This sharp rise in immigration has caused many people to question the policies on immigration and call for more restrictive laws. Many of the debates about immigration policy in the United States center around the economic factors involved with immigration, which is not surprising, because the strong economy is the biggest pull factor for immigrants.

Immigrants from China helped the U.S. economy in the 1800s, primarily by providing manual labor for the railroad industry. Such is the case in this photograph taken in California circa 1890.

IMMIGRATION HELPS THE ECONOMY

People who believe that immigration is good for the economy like to point out how immigration has always helped the economy in the past. Historically, businesses encourage immigration, as it provides them with a larger workforce and a greater number of job applicants to choose from for any given job. In fact, times of heavy immigration tend to also be periods of economic growth and prosperity. The unlimited supply of workers allows businesses to keep production costs down, which means that they can afford to charge less for their goods and services. The lower prices, in turn, mean that Americans can afford to purchase more, which raises the standard of living.

THE MELTING POT VERSUS THE SALAD BOWL

One of the concerns that some critics of immigration have is that immigrants don't seem to be "melting" into the melting pot of American culture as much as they used to. The term "melting pot" came from a 1908 play of the same title. The play, written by Israel Zangwill, was a modernization of the Romeo and Juliet story, romanticizing how younger generations of immigrants from different European countries were setting their family's ethnic traditions and resentments aside and coming together to create a new American culture from a blend of many different cultures. Today, some critics of immigration worry that modern immigrants don't "melt" or "assimilate" into general American culture very well. Rather, there is a concern that many immigrants prefer to congregate together in the cities that they settle in, socializing only among themselves, speaking only their native languages, and preserving their native cultures. However, many sociologists don't necessarily see this failure to assimilate as a negative thing. They point out that the circumstances for modern immigrants are different: at the time that the term "melting pot" was coined, most immigrants at least shared a general European heritage, while now immigrants come from nations around the globe. Sociologists suggest that instead of a melting pot, today's immigration is more like a salad bowl, where different ingredients are brought together to create a wonderful whole, while still retaining the characteristics that made them separate ingredients in their own right.

During the Great Period of Immigration at the turn of the last century, immigration was thought to be one of the main contributing factors toward the growth and success of American industry. Millions of young, energetic workers came to America and helped build the nation's new railroads, factories, mills, and highways. Without the help of the immigrants, many American businesses would not have had enough employees to survive, and the country would not have been able to grow as quickly and as strongly as it did.

IMMIGRANTS FILL THE HIGHS AND LOWS

Another pro-immigration argument is that most immigrants tend to find jobs at the two extremes of the economic spectrum. In the past, the majority of immigrants tended to fill manual-labor jobs, usually in service or agricultural industries. Immigrants are historically willing to work hard at these low-wage jobs because of the high standard of living in the United States, which means that even though the wages for these jobs might be low by American standards, they are still often higher than they were in the country that the immigrant came from. The general argument in favor of the immigrants is that they will "take the jobs that no one else will take"; in other words, the low-wage service industry or agricultural jobs that most Americans don't want. Some economists argue that this allows the native-born Americans to move up the economic ladder and be considered for higher-paying jobs.

In addition, recently a higher percentage of immigrants have been filling jobs at the top of the economic ladder in high-tech industries such as computer science, biotechnology, medicine, and engineering. This is due in part to the fact that businesses in these areas are growing faster than our own native population can keep up with, and we can't supply enough of our own workers to fill all of these new jobs. The use of immigrant labor in these industries is helping to keep America growing in these areas, which in turn keeps us technologically competitive with the rest of the world.

IMMIGRANTS DON'T HELP THE ECONOMY

However, not everyone agrees with these economic arguments in favor of immigration. Many economists point out that immigration and economic growth are not necessarily tied to one another. Many countries that severely restrict immigration, such as Japan, have still historically experienced periods of very strong economic growth. Further, except for the Great Depression in the 1930s, the period from 1914 to 1965 was one of America's greatest periods of prosperity, and it was also a period of the most restrictive limitations on immigration because of the quota system.

Although businesses encourage immigration as a way to continue to have a large pool of workers to choose from, some economists point out that the endless supply of cheap labor keeps the minimum wage down in the United States. Businesses are not forced to pay their workers more if there is always someone else (usually an immigrant) who is willing to do the same job for lower pay.

A Hispanic worker in the Napa Valley area of California carries a basket of grapes at a winery. Many immigrants find jobs in the agriculture and service industries.

People who would like to limit immigration also do not agree with the idea that immigrants are filling the jobs that Americans do not want to do. Instead, they argue that there are plenty of Americans who would like to fill those service industry and agriculture jobs, but the wages for the jobs are kept so low by the overabundance of immigrant labor that they can't support themselves and their families on the salary. If there were fewer people competing for those jobs, industries would be forced to raise the minimum wage in order to find workers willing to do the jobs. Once the minimum wage went up, more native-born Americans would be willing to work in those positions. This would eliminate the need for immigrant help. Further, America is currently experiencing one of the highest percentages of unemployment in years. Many people argue that this is because the immigrants are adding too many people into the workforce, and there simply aren't enough American jobs for everybody.

IMMIGRANTS FILL MORE LOWS THAN HIGHS

Many people do not accept the argument that immigrants are contributing to the growth of the high-tech industries in this country, either. They point out that even though some immigrants are coming into America to fill gaps in the high-tech industries, our current immigration policy is biased more heavily toward family reunification-based immigration, rather than on skills-based immigration. This means that the overwhelming majority of people who come to America are not being admitted in because they have high-tech skills, but instead because they have relatives already in this country. Many of these people are not any more highly educated or highly skilled than the average native worker, and oftentimes they are less. This is a problem, since American industry is moving toward a technological base and away from the former industrial and agricultural base.

As you can see, economic factors are a major point of argument when it comes to the debate on immigration. Many people believe that the economy needs immigrants to grow and thrive, while many others believe that immigrants actually depress the country economically. But although the economy is

A lab technician works in a DNA sequencing laboratory. There is debate about how many immigrants are coming to America to work in high-tech industries such as this one.

one of the greatest factors in the argument over immigration, it is by far not the only factor. There are also many people who are concerned about the social, environmental, cultural, and global impact of immigration to the United States.

Chapter 3

The Debate on Social Services and Global Policy

Another major argument about U.S. immigration concerns the impact that immigrants have on social service programs. America, like most economically advanced countries, has a system of social services and public assistance available to its citizens. Some of the largest social service programs include welfare, public schools, and Medicaid. All of these programs are funded, in major part, from tax dollars that Americans pay to the federal and state governments. Many people feel that these social service programs are being stressed and overtaxed. Often, they point to the rise of the immigrant population in the United States as the cause of the stress.

Pictured here are students in a Chicago public school. Some people feel that the large number of children of immigrants, especially illegal immigrants, is threatening the public school systems in the United States.

IMMIGRANTS ARE A DRAIN ON THE SYSTEM

Critics of immigration argue that immigrants are creating a burden on social service programs because they use more social services than they are able to pay for in tax dollars. Legal immigrants are eligible for many welfare programs after they have lived in the United States for five years, including food stamps and Medicaid programs. While illegal immigrants are not eligible to apply for most welfare programs, any children that they have that are born in the United States are eligible, even if the parents are still illegal. Further, the children of both legal and illegal immigrants are allowed to attend public schools, and both legal and illegal immigrants are able to receive emergency medical care.

Unfortunately, when immigrants utilize the social services that they are eligible for, it presents a huge financial problem for several states in the country. Although the bulk of tax money is paid to the federal government, many of the services that immigrants are eligible for are those that are funded primarily by the state governments. Currently, states are having a hard time funding their social services programs because of the large strain that the immigrant population is placing on their systems.

IMMIGRANTS DON'T DRAIN THE SYSTEM

On the other hand, critics of these arguments point out that immigrants pay taxes just like native citizens do, and as such should be given the same services for their tax dollars that native citizens receive. While it is true that immigrants on the whole pay less in taxes than the average American, the critics argue that it isn't the fault of the immigrants; federal taxes are based on income, and generally immigrants have a lower income, so naturally they pay less in taxes.

Further, although it is true that a higher proportion of immigrants apply for welfare programs than native-born Americans do, supporters of immigration argue that the proportions are unfairly represented because refugees and the elderly are included in with the immigrant numbers. Immigrants who qualify for refugee status in the United States do not have to wait five years in order to be eligible for welfare, and refugees

Pictured here are protesters at an anti-illegal immigration rally in Washington, D.C. Illegal immigrants are still able to receive emergency health care, although they do not pay any federal taxes.

tend to come to this country with very little in the way of personal belongings, job skills, or education. Many of them need welfare in order to survive and usually apply for welfare immediately upon entering the United States. In addition, the current U.S. immigration policy of family reunification means that immigrants are able to bring elderly parents and grandparents here to live with them. These older people have a harder time finding employment, and as a result are more likely to have to apply for public assistance of some type.

Without the refugees and older immigrants factored into the proportions, those in favor of immigration argue that the average immigrant actually requires less public assistance than most native-born Americans. Further, immigrants are not eligible for Social Security benefits unless they become naturalized citizens, so many immigrants pay the federal government tax money that funds Social Security programs that they will never be able to use.

As for the argument that a few states unfairly carry the burden of providing services for immigrants, supporters of immigration argue that the burden is not the fault of the immigrant, but of the tax system, which doesn't properly support the states. Allowing immigrants to have access to state-funded programs such as public education only helps to increase the potential for the children of immigrants to get better, higher-paying jobs, which in turn means that they will eventually move into a higher tax bracket and pay more taxes. This gradual improvement of the standard of living for immigrant families will help to support the social programs in the long run.

U.S. IMMIGRATION BENEFITS THE GLOBE

For the most part, the United States has historically enjoyed a relatively good reputation globally. Many foreigners tend to think of America in terms of the American dream. America is seen as being a land of opportunity, with a very high standard of living and an abundance of freedoms. This is not the case in many other areas of the globe, especially in third world countries where poverty and oppression are more likely to be the norm. Because of this, many Americans believe that they bear a large responsibility to set a global standard and to try to help improve the rest of the world. Improving the quality of life on a global scale would also help to improve life in the United States, since everyone in the world would benefit from a

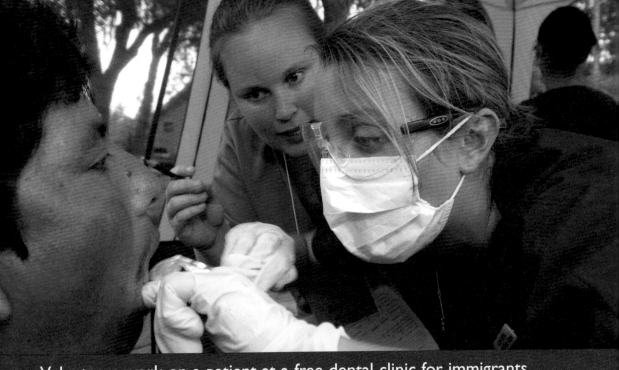

Volunteers work on a patient at a free dental clinic for immigrants. Many people believe that U.S. citizens have a social obligation to help immigrants better their standard of living.

peaceful, economically productive, and technologically innovative global environment.

According to those with this viewpoint, the United States can help not only by taking in refugees in need, but also by providing an education to temporary immigrants who come to America to learn methods and skills that they can apply to their own governments and industries when they return to their home countries. In this way, the United States can help to stabilize third world countries and raise the global standard of living.

Further, it is in America's best interest to continue to provide opportunities to immigrants because it allows the country to continue to have a good reputation with the rest of the world.

When immigration is part of the foreign policy, it creates good will amongst other nations.

U.S. IMMIGRATION HARMS THE GLOBE

On the other hand, many Americans don't agree that the United States should feel as if it is responsible for improving the rest of the world. They point out that there are limits to what the United States can do to help solve world problems, especially when it has so many problems of its own that it must fix first. As a country, they argue, the United States has a larger responsibility to think of itself first and to concentrate on its native-born citizens before inviting others to come to America.

In addition, many people point out that immigrants from third world countries who come to America for an education very rarely return back to their home countries to help improve conditions there. On the contrary, over half decide to stay in the United States. This actually does more harm than good to third world countries, as it causes a "brain drain" in those countries, meaning the best and the brightest citizens leave the country instead of staying to help improve conditions.

The criticism against taking in global refugees who come to America seeking political or religious freedom is similar. When the United States allows immigration for refugees who come from countries with civil rights violations, it means that the opponents of corrupt and evil regimes are allowed to escape the country, rather than being forced to stay and overthrow the corrupt government. Opponents of immigration argue that if

THE MARIEL BOATLIFT

One of the best-known examples of the United States acting as a place of refuge happened between April 15 and October 31, 1980, when up to 125,000 Cuban citizens left Cuba to come to the United States. This event, known as the Mariel Boatlift because the refugees left from Cuba's Mariel Harbor, has been a topic of argument among sociologists since it happened. Since 1959, Cuba has been ruled by Fidel Castro, a Communist dictator who has maintained a policy of closed borders, preventing his citizens from emigrating to other nations. However, in 1977, the economy of Cuba began to take a downturn, and some Cubans became increasingly dissatisfied with conditions there. By 1980, a group of citizens demonstrated against the government by storming the Peruvian embassy in Cuba, demanding that Peru take them in as refugees. In response, Fidel Castro announced that for a short period of time, anyone who wanted to leave Cuba would be permitted to go. People wishing to emigrate were told to go to Mariel Harbor, where they were shoved onto crowded boats and set into the ocean. The United States ended up taking the refugees in, which created a lot of goodwill between the U.S. government and the large population of Cuban immigrants who were already living in the United States. However, it is debated that although the United States was able to play the role of "the good guy" in this instance, Fidel Castro could have been playing the role of the "evil genius," since he was able to quickly stop what might have turned into a revolution against him, and at the same time, he was able to rid his country of 125,000 dissidents.

A fishing boat full of Cuban refugees heads toward Key West on June 4, 1980. Boats such as this were packed with refugees during the Mariel Boatlift.

America did not allow so many immigrants in, perhaps people would be less likely to leave corrupt or poverty-stricken third world countries, and instead would stay in their homelands and work harder to improve conditions there.

Finally, there are many who think that America's reputation as being a compassionate nation is actually working against it, as people take advantage of the country's compassion and willingness to accept immigrants. The arguments about immigration and the foreign policy of compassion were a major topic of debate after America was attacked on its home soil on September 11, 2001.

Chapter 4

Our Security and Our Borders

On September 11, 2001, nineteen terrorists from four Middle Eastern countries hijacked four commercial U.S. airliners. Two of the airliners hit the World Trade Center's twin towers in New York City, one airliner hit the Pentagon outside Washington, D.C., and one airliner, thought to be bound for the White House, crashed in a field in Pennsylvania before it reached its intended destination. Of the nineteen hijackers, at least three were illegal immigrants. Several of the others had come to the United States on fraudulent student visas.

In the wake of this attack, known as 9/11, there was immediate concern about America's immigration policies and the safety of its borders. Many Americans became

A former U.S. immigrant returns to Pakistan in 2003 after the U.S. government deported him. Following 9/11, the immigration visas of Middle Eastern immigrants were subject to much closer inspection.

wary of immigrants in general, and there was a large percentage of the population that began arguing for more conservative immigration policies. Many of the debates about immigration that began on 9/11 are still being argued today.

IMMIGRATION LAW AS A COUNTERTERRORISM TOOL

One of the areas of debate concerns whether or not the government should be able to use U.S. immigration policies as weapons in the war against terrorism. There are many critics who say that America uses standard immigration law to discriminate against Muslim immigrants. These critics say that people who immigrate to America from Islamic countries are often subjected to a much more thorough investigation than others and are more likely to be detained or deported because of technical errors or minor mistakes in their immigration paperwork. They argue that the practice of being overly vigilant of Muslim immigrants encourages persecution based on race and religion.

Despite these arguments, the government defends the practice of using immigration law as a tool in the War on Terror. Immigration officials point out that they aren't deporting people without just cause, they are simply being more vigilant in enforcing the laws that already exist. Further, they claim that being more cautious and thorough in examining the immigration documents of people coming from countries that are known to harbor terrorists is justified following 9/11.

Terrorists are difficult to catch because law enforcement officials are trying to identify who the terrorists might be before they actually strike. People who are intending to engage in terrorist activity might not have broken any laws yet, so law enforcement officials usually have no basis for detaining suspected terrorists until they commit an act of terrorism. However, government officials say that one of the mistakes that many terrorists do routinely make is immigration fraud, which makes immigration law one of the only legal ways to deal with and detain suspected terrorists.

However, it has been said that people who apply to enter legally are the least of our problems when it comes to possible terrorism. Instead, many people identify our country's porous borders at Mexico and Canada as the real problem. Terrorists,

IIRA/IRA

Muslim immigrants are not the only people who are feeling the effects of post-9/11 immigration policies. Another side effect of increased vigilance is that laws that had been largely ignored in the past are now being much more strictly enforced. Specifically, a law passed in 1996 called the Illegal Immigration Reform and Immigrant Responsibility Act (known as IIRA/IRA) has many immigrants worried. The act mandates that immigrants with any criminal record—even minor offenses—should be deported. Further, the act is applied retroactively, which means that it impacts immigrants who committed minor offenses years ago. However, this law was not strictly enforced until after 9/11. Since then, there have been several outcries concerning IIRA/IRA prosecutions that seem unfairly strict. For example, a 2004 article in the *New Statesman* shared the story of a young mother of two children in Georgia, who as a baby had been adopted from Germany. Her adoptive American parents had accidentally forgotten to formally file papers to have her citizenship changed, and when she discovered the oversight and filed the papers as an adult, her case was flagged due to a conviction of misdemeanor battery—the result of a hair-pulling incident with an old boyfriend. As a result, she was in danger of being deported back to Germany without her children, despite the fact that she did not speak a word of German. Luckily for her, she won an appeal and was allowed to stay. However, in a post-9/11 world of heightened security, not everyone is so lucky.

they say, are less likely to apply for entrance to the United States with fraudulent papers than they are likely to simply illegally sneak over the border. This brings us to the debate over border control.

THE UNITED STATES' RELATIONSHIP WITH MEXICO

The border between the United States and Canada is 3,145 miles (5,061 kilometers) long, and the border between the United States and Mexico is 1,951 miles (3,140 km) long. Despite the fact that Canada's border is longer and both borders are equally porous, the debate about U.S. border control tends to center around the border with Mexico. This is in part because it is the most frequently crossed international border in the world, with an estimated 350 million people legally crossing it every year, according to the U.S. embassy in Mexico. It is also in part due to the fact that the United States experiences more instances of illegal crossing at the Mexican border than it does at the Canadian border.

When it comes to the issue of immigration, the United States' relationship with Mexico is historically problematic. The difference between the income of the average American citizen and the income of the average Mexican citizen is the largest income gap between two neighboring nations in the world. This creates a huge economic pull factor for Mexican citizens, many of whom already have relatives living in America. Mexican citizens now account for 30 percent of all legal immigrants and 78 percent of all illegal immigrants in the United States.

Mexican immigration to the United States was encouraged during World War II, when Mexicans were brought in to help with agriculture production while American workers were fighting overseas. This practice continued into the 1960s and established the basis for future Mexican immigration to the United States. This basis was added to substantially in 1986 when President Ronald Reagan signed the Immigration Reform and Control Act. This act was intended to decrease the number of illegal immigrants coming into the country from Mexico by making it illegal for a company to knowingly hire an illegal immigrant.

However, critics of the law say that the act backfired because it also gave amnesty to the 2.7 million illegal immigrants who were already living in the United States at the time. Granting citizenship to the illegal immigrants that were already in the United States gave potentially illegal immigrants hope. Further, it established more Mexican immigrant families in the United States—families that could now apply to bring even more relatives in under the family reunification policy.

THE RUN FOR THE BORDER

Currently, the number of immigrants who try to cross the Mexican border illegally is growing every year, creating a new criminal culture. According to the U.S. government, between 300,000 and 400,000 people try to cross the border illegally every year. People calling themselves "coyotes" are making a living out of smuggling potentially illegal immigrants across the border, sometimes safely and sometimes not. The Mexican

Immigrants attempt to illegally enter the United States by swimming across the New River, a river separating Mexico from the United States. The New River is one of the nation's most polluted rivers.

government reports that an estimated 400 or so people die yearly trying to illegally cross the border.

Considering these statistics, most people agree that there are significant problems with the state of the U.S.-Mexico border. However, what hasn't been agreed on yet is what should be done to solve the problems. Some people favor a no-tolerance policy and argue that the government should spend more time searching for and immediately deporting illegals. Others point out that as long as there are jobs to be had for illegal immigrants in the United States, they will keep coming right back over the border even after they've been deported. Besides, many argue that with an estimated twelve million illegal immigrants currently in the United States, finding and deporting them all would be an impossible task.

One argument is that because jobs are the major pull factor for illegal immigration across the Mexican border, it makes the

A volunteer scans the horizon, searching for illegal immigrants coming over the Mexican border. Many volunteer organizations have been created to assist the U.S. Border Patrol in securing the borders.

most sense to target the American businesses that hire illegal immigrants. Vigilantly enforcing the laws against employing illegals would reduce the number of jobs available to illegal immigrants. However, it is very difficult to prove that a business has knowingly hired an illegal immigrant. Further, some think that other pull factors would still draw illegal immigrants into the United States. For instance, the policy that all children born in the United States are automatically granted U.S. citizenship status regardless of the immigration status of their parents would continue to be a significant pull factor for families.

Finally, there are those who think that the problem of illegal immigration at the Mexican border can be solved by more vigilant patrolling of the border itself. Solutions such as an

THE MINUTEMAN PROJECT

The Minuteman Project, Inc. is a controversial group that describes itself as being "a neighborhood watch on the border." Founded in 2004, the group enlists concerned citizens to help the U.S. Border Patrol watch the border with Mexico. Members of the project routinely patrol the border looking for illegal immigrants and then call the Border Patrol when they spot illegal activity. In addition to patrolling the borders, the group also lobbies the government for tighter immigration control and has helped to build fences on private property along the length of the Mexican border. The group has expanded to watch the U.S. border with Canada as well.

Reaction to the Minuteman Project is mixed. President George W. Bush has referred to the group members as being "vigilantes." Some people have suggested that the project accepts skinheads and members of the American Nazi Party into their membership—an accusation that the project members strongly deny. However, some political figures, such as California governor Arnold Schwarzenegger, have praised the project and said that they do a terrific job.

The Minuteman Project should not be confused with the Minuteman Civil Defense Corps, another separate, smaller organization that also uses volunteers to patrol the Mexican border.

increase of U.S. Border Patrol officers, the deployment of National Guard troops at the border, and even the idea of building a wall along the border have been suggested. However, others argue that the border itself is too long and too unpopulated to fully patrol, and a fence or wall would take too much money to build and maintain. Furthermore, in the 1990s when the government increased border enforcement at the most traveled sections of the border, it simply resulted in a greater number of deaths, as illegal immigrants tried to cross the border in increasingly remote and dangerous places.

Because the Mexican border is one of the biggest problem areas in the debate on American immigration, it has become a hot-button issue in American politics.

Chapter 5

The Political Future of the Immigration Debate

Not surprisingly, the two opposing political parties in the United States have two very different attitudes toward immigration, although they do agree on a few basic points. Both parties agree that illegal immigration is a problem in the United States, and that immigration policies need to be reformed. However, the Democratic Party has traditionally held more liberal views toward immigration. The Democrats' platform on immigration focuses more on attempting to legalize the illegal immigrants already in the United States, giving them a path to eventually become legal citizens. The Democrats also believe that family reunification should continue to be the overriding emphasis of immigration policies.

President George W. Bush introduces his "guest worker" plan for immigration policy at a press conference in 2004. His political party, the Republican Party, did not entirely approve of his plan.

While the Republican Party has historically leaned toward policies that support business and capitalism in America, its stance on immigration has shifted some in recent years. Although it can be argued that immigration is good for business because it supplies the United States with a larger pool of prospective workers and keeps production costs down, the Republican Party does not support liberal immigration policies.

The Republican platform on immigration calls for tougher border control measures and tougher enforcement of current immigration laws in order to deport illegal immigrants. In recent years, many Republicans have made immigration a major issue in their campaigns, calling for a crackdown on illegal immigrants and refusing any amnesty programs for illegals currently in the country. Republicans also advocate moving away from the family reunification policies and more toward policies that favor highly skilled foreign workers.

THE GUEST WORKER PLAN

Surprisingly, however, when it comes to immigration, President George W. Bush did not exactly follow the platform of his Republican Party. Instead, Bush advocated a "guest worker" plan for immigration. Bush's guest worker plan basically would have permitted both new immigrants and illegal immigrants already in the United States to apply for a guest worker visa, which would have allowed them to work legally in the United States for up to three years. After that time, a guest worker would have had the option to apply for citizenship if he or she wanted to, but would not have been shown any favoritism in obtaining citizenship. Guest workers who did not apply for and receive citizenship would have had to agree to leave the United States immediately after their guest worker visas expired.

However, under Bush's proposal, the guest workers would have been granted some rights that previously only citizens were entitled to. Guest workers would have been able to receive Social Security benefits while they were employed in the United States, and they would also have been protected under U.S. labor laws. This would have ensured that they would have earned at least minimum wage, which is a higher wage than many illegal immigrants now receive in the United States. In addition, guest workers would have also been able to come and go across the border freely without fear of being detained or deported, which is a freedom that most illegal immigrants currently in the United States do not have. Guest workers would also have been given U.S.-sponsored retirement benefits that could have only been redeemed in their home countries, which would have given the guest workers added incentive to actually leave the country after their visas expired.

For their part, the American businesses that hired guest workers would have been required to prove that they had hired the workers only after they had made an attempt to hire native-born American workers first. Supporters of Bush's plan point out that allowing guest workers into the country still would have benefited American business and industry by continuing to keep the labor force large and diverse.

Supporters of Bush's guest worker program also argue that it would have allowed the overworked U.S. Border Patrol to shift much of its attention away from searching for illegal immigrants and toward being more watchful for terrorist breaches of the border.

CRITICISMS OF BUSH'S PLAN

Because Bush's plan differed somewhat from his political party's stance on immigration, his guest worker proposal drew criticism from both Republicans and Democrats. Republican opposition centered on the fact that the plan would have been open to current illegal immigrants in the United States, and many Republicans view this as giving undeserved legal status to people who have knowingly broken U.S. laws. Republicans also argued that the plan did nothing to address the strain

Protesters attend a demonstration against a proposed immigration bill. Protests both for and against immigration are becoming more common as immigration becomes a widely debated political issue.

that immigration is causing on the social service programs in the United States. They argue that even with the guest workers earning minimum wage and paying taxes, the fact that they were still most likely to be in the lowest tax bracket meant that they would have continued to use more social services than they would have been able to repay in taxes.

Democrats, on the other hand, faulted the plan for favoring businesses over immigrants. They argued that the plan ultimately would have only benefited American businesses because it did not help guest workers move toward citizenship in any way. Rather, it would have created a group of temporary workers in the United States who wouldn't have had any greater hope of being granted citizenship than they would

A NATIONAL EMPLOYMENT ELIGIBILITY VERIFICATION SYSTEM

One of the few elements that was shared by the 2005 House immigration bill and the 2006 Senate bill was that both contained a provision for establishing a national Employment Eligibility Verification System (or EEVS). Currently, although employers are required by law to verify if a job applicant is legal to work in the United States, so many different documents qualify as proof of legality that employers have trouble being familiar with them all, and counterfeits can be easily obtained by illegal immigrants. An EEVS is a computer-based system that allows employers to check the immigration status of every candidate for a job by verifying the applicant's Social Security number directly with the U.S. government. Critics of EEVS point out that illegal immigrants could simply counterfeit the documents necessary to obtain a Social Security card and still beat the system. Also, the cost of the EEVS could be prohibitive, as some experts have estimated that creating a nationwide system could cost in the hundreds of millions of dollars. Even so, without an accurate national verification system in place, it is very difficult to hold employers accountable for knowingly employing illegal immigrants.

have had before the program began. Democrats feared that this would have been the same as creating a group of "second-class" citizens, who although they were here legally, were not given any assurance that they could have ever been allowed to permanently stay in America.

THREE IMMIGRATION BILLS

Because of opposition to the guest worker plan by both Democrats and Republicans, Bush's plan in its entirety was never translated into legislation. However, this doesn't mean that immigration reform has not been a topic of current legislation. On the contrary, in the last few years, three major bills have been passed concerning immigration. The first piece of legislation was passed by the Republican-held House of Representatives in 2005. This controversial bill focused on border security, changing illegal immigration from being a civil offense punishable by deportment, to a criminal offense punishable by jail time. It also made the act of aiding an illegal immigrant a criminal offense and contained a provision for the funding for new fencing to be constructed along the Mexican border. This bill did not get the Senate approval that it needed in order to become a law, however.

A year later, the U.S. Senate passed another immigration reform bill. The Senate bill was a bipartisan bill that was authored by both Democrat and Republican senators, and it included elements of both party's immigration platforms. The Senate bill provided for a guest worker program that was similar to the one proposed by President Bush, but that allowed

An estimated 125,000 demonstrators marched in support of immigrants in Phoenix, Arizona, in 2006. The debate about immigration is most active in southeastern states with higher Hispanic populations.

for a clear path to citizenship for illegal immigrants currently in the United States. In addition, it also included many of the strict border enforcement provisions that Republicans wanted. The House Republicans blocked this Senate bill, and instead introduced a third bill that appropriated more money for border security and called for 700 miles of fencing to be built along the Mexican border. However, this new bill did not call for the criminalization of giving aid to an illegal immigrant, nor did it propose to make illegal immigration a felony offense. Without these elements, the Senate agreed to pass this third bill and it was signed into law by President Bush in October of 2006.

THE DEBATE CONTINUES

However, because this new law did not provide for any substantial reform of immigration law, U.S. immigration policy continues to be a hot political topic. Opinion polls of American citizens have shown that as the numbers of immigrants continue to rise, immigration reform is becoming one of the top concerns of voters. Experts predict that in the coming years immigration will most likely be one of the key factors in elections across the country.

It is obvious that immigration policy is a very complex issue with many different factors to consider. A good debate on immigration policy should take into account economic arguments, social service arguments, and arguments concerning the issues of border control and national security, just to name a few issues. However, fundamentally, the underlying debate about immigration remains the same as it has been since the foundation of the country.

To what extent is America expected to live up to the lines of poetry written by Emma Lazarus more than 100 years ago? To what extent do we want to be the country of the American dream? To what extent are we really a great melting pot in which all cultures blend peacefully together and unending refuge is granted to the tired, the poor, and the huddled masses yearning to breathe free?

And to what extent is that idea just unrealistic, impossible lines of poetry?

Timeline

1790 The Naturalization Act grants U.S. citizenship to "free, white persons" who have lived in the United States for at least two years; Congress authorizes the first census, which records the population of the United States at nearly four million.

1870 A new naturalization law restricts citizenship to only people of European or African descent.

1882 The Chinese Exclusion Act prohibits Asians from obtaining U.S. citizenship.

1891 The first U.S. Bureau of Immigration is established. It falls under the direction of the U.S. Treasury Department.

1900 With forty-five states in the union, the census records that the population of the United States is seventy-six million people.

1907 The highest year for immigration through Ellis Island, with over one million immigrants; an agreement with Japan allows Japanese workers to immigrate to Hawaii, although they are barred from coming to the U.S. mainland.

1918 Quota systems are put into place that allow a greater number of British and western European immigrants to come to the United States.

1940 The Chinese Exclusion Act is repealed.

1965 The Immigration Act of 1965 changes the quota system so that immigration policy no longer favors Europeans.

1980 The Refugee Act allows ten million immigrants to be granted legal citizenship.

1986 The Immigration Reform and Control Act grants amnesty to 2.7 million illegal immigrants in the United States.

1996 The Immigration Welfare and Reform Act reduces the rights and social benefits of illegal immigrants and strengthens border enforcement.

1997 The Illegal Immigration Reform and Immigrant Responsibility Act allocates money for more border patrol agents and for construction of fences on the U.S.-Mexico border.

2000 The 2000 census records the U.S. population at more than 260 million.

2001 Following 9/11, the USA Patriot Act grants the government more power to investigate and deport immigrants.

2003 The Department of Homeland Security takes over the Immigration and Naturalization Service.

2004 President Bush introduces his "guest worker" initiative.

2005 The U.S House of Representatives passes H.R.4437, a bill calling for the criminalization of illegal immigration and for money to strengthen the U.S. Border Patrol.

May 2006 The U.S. Senate passes S.2611, a bill that calls for a modified guest worker program and the strengthening of the border between the United States and Mexico.

October 2006 President Bush signs into law a bill that omits the criminalization of illegal immigration and a guest worker program, but that retains provisions to strengthen the U.S.-Mexico border by building fences.

Glossary

animosity Ill will or resentment that may lead to active hostility.

assimilate To take in or make similar.

brain drain The term used for talented, bright, intellectual citizens leaving their homeland to immigrate and add such talent to a new country, rather than staying and trying to improve conditions in their homeland.

colossus Someone of exceptional strength, power, and reputation; a giant. A statue of gigantic size and proportions.

deport To send out of the country.

detain To keep from proceeding or to keep in custody.

dissident A person who disagrees with an established political system or religious belief.

emigrate To leave one's country to live elsewhere.

family reunification Immigration policy that favors immigration of people who already have family members living in the United States.

Great Period of Immigration The era between the mid-1800s and the early 1900s when over thirty million immigrants came to the United States, mostly from Europe.

immigrate To come to a country that is not one's homeland, with the intention of establishing permanent residence.

Know-Nothing Party A political party that formed in the 1840s in New York and ran on the platform of restricting the rights of Irish immigrants.

Glossary

Medicaid A federally funded program administered by individual states that provides health care and related services to persons who meet the eligibility requirements.

migration To move from one country to another.

minimum wage The minimum amount of money per hour that an employee can legally be paid by his or her employer.

naturalization The process required to be admitted as a citizen.

porous Capable of being entered or penetrated.

pull factor Those advantages of another country that persuade a person to want to immigrate.

push factor Those disadvantages or hardships in a person's homeland that cause him or her to want to emigrate.

quota system The prescribed number or limit of persons who, in the case of U.S. immigration at one time, could immigrate from their particular country of origin to the United States.

refugee Someone who has left his or her home country for another due to danger or fear of persecution.

Social Security A federal program that provides money to elderly and disabled people.

vigilant Alert or watchful.

visa A document or stamp affixed to a person's passport authorizing entry for specific purposes for a certain length of time.

welfare Economic assistance provided by the government for persons in need.

For More Information

American Immigrant Control Foundation (AICF)
P.O. Box 525
Monterey, VA 24465
(703) 468-2022
Web site: http://www.aicfoundation.com

American Immigration Lawyers Association (AILA)
1400 I Street NW, Suite 1200
Washington, DC 20005
(202) 216-2400
Web site: http://www.aila.org

Americans for Immigration Control (AIC)
725 Second Street NE, Suite 307
Washington, DC 20002
(202) 543-3719
Web site: http://www.immigrationcontrol.com

Center for Immigration Studies
1522 K Street NW, Suite 820
Washington, DC 20005
(202) 466-8185
Web site: http://www.cis.org

For More Information

Federation for American Immigrant Reform (FAIR)
1666 Connecticut Avenue NW, Suite 400
Washington, DC 20009
(202) 328-7004
Web site: http://www.fairus.org

National Council of La Raza (NCLA)
1111 19th Street NW, Suite 1000
Washington, DC 20036
(202) 289-1380
Web site: http://www.nclr.org

National Immigration Forum
220 I Street NE, Suite 220
Washington, DC 20002
(202) 544-0004
Web site: http://www.immigrationforum.org

National Network for Immigrants and Refugee Rights (NNIRR)
310 Eighth Street, Suite 307
Oakland, CA 94607
(510) 465-1984
Web site: http://www.nnirr.org

Negative Population Growth, Inc. (NPG)
1717 Massachusetts Avenue NW, Suite 101
Washington, DC 20036

(202) 667-8950

Web site: http://www.npg.org

U.S. Committee for Refugees and Immigrants (USCRI)
1717 Massachusetts Avenue NW, 2nd Floor
Washington, DC 20036
(202) 347-3507
Web site: http://www.refugees.org

Web Sites

Due to the changing nature of Internet links, Rosen Publishing has developed an online list of Web sites related to the subject of this book. This site is updated regularly. Please use this link to access the list:

http://www.rosenlinks.com/ad/adpi

For Further Reading

Ashabranner, Brent K. *Still a Nation of Immigrants*. New York, NY: Dutton Books, 1993.

Bode, Janet. *New Kids in Town: Oral Histories of Immigrant Teens*. New York, NY: Scholastic, 1989.

Bode, Janet. *The Colors of Freedom: Immigrant Stories*. Danbury, CT: Franklin Watts, 1999.

Cothran, Helen, ed. *Current Controversies: Illegal Immigration*. San Diego, CA: Greenhaven Press, 2001.

Freedman, Russell. *Immigrant Kids*. New York, NY: Puffin Books, 1980.

Gallo, Donald R. ed. *First Crossing: Stories About Teen Immigrants*. Cambridge, MA: Candlewick Press, 2004.

Haerens, Margaret, ed. *Opposing Viewpoints: Illegal Immigration*. San Diego, CA: Greenhaven Press, 2006.

Kosof, Anna. *Living in Two Worlds: The Immigrant Children's Experience*. New York, NY: Twenty-first Century Books, 1996.

Levine, Herbert M. *American Issues Debated: Immigration*. Austin, TX: Raintree Steck-Vaughn, 1998.

Reimers, David M. *A Land of Immigrants*. Broomall, PA: Chelsea House, 1995.

Senker, Cath. *Immigrants and Refugees*. Milwaukee, WI: World Almanac Library, 2005.

Williams, Mary E. *Opposing Viewpoints Series: Immigration*. San Diego, CA: Greenhaven Press, 2004.

Bibliography

Baicker, Karen. *Primary Sources Teaching Kit: Immigration*. New York, NY: Scholastic Press, 2003.

Bell, Jeffrey. "The Coming Immigration Deal; Congress Will Follow the Polls." *Weekly Standard*. June 19, 2006, p. 38.

Campo-Flores, Arian. "America's Divide." *Newsweek*. April 10, 2006, p. 28.

Cothran, Helen, ed. *Current Controversies: Illegal Immigration*. San Diego, CA: Greenhaven Press, 2001.

Davis, Stephen. "Deported from America." *New Statesman*. November 22, 2004, pp. 14–17.

Facts on File World News Digest. "The House and Senate Immigration Reform Bills: Highlights." May 25, 2006. Retrieved November 6, 2006 (http://www.facts.com).

Facts on File Issues and Controversies. "Immigration Law and Terrorism." July 8, 2005. Retrieved November 6, 2006 (http://www.facts.com).

Facts on File Issues and Controversies. "Immigration Services Reform." June 21, 2002. Retrieved November 6, 2006 (http://www.facts.com).

Facts on File Issues and Controversies. "National Anthem." May 26, 2006. Retrieved November 6, 2006 (http://www.facts.com).

Facts on File World News Digest. "2000 Census: Racial, Ethnic Minority Populations Surge." May 10, 2001. Retrieved November 6, 2006 (http://www.facts.com).

Bibliography

Facts on File Issues and Controversies. "Update: Immigration."
January 30, 2004. Retrieved November 6, 2006
(http://www.facts.com).

Facts on File Issues and Controversies. "Update: U.S.-Mexico
Border Enforcement." July 7, 2006. Retrieved November 6,
2006 (http://www.facts.com).

Facts on File World News Digest. "US Senate Passes Immigration
Reform Bill." May 25, 2006. Retrieved November 6, 2006
(http://www.facts.com).

Haerens, Margaret, ed. *Opposing Viewpoints: Illegal Immigration.*
San Diego, CA: Greenhaven Press, 2006.

Klein, Joe. "Bush Is Smart on the Border—and the G.O.P. Isn't."
Time. May 29, 2006, p. 25.

Levine, Herbert M. *American Issues Debated: Immigration.* Austin, TX:
Raintree Steck-Vaughn, 1998.

Lilleyman, Sarah. "Illegals? Not in These Towns." *Time.* July 31,
2006, p. 16.

Reimers, David M. *A Land of Immigrants.* Broomall, PA: Chelsea
House, 1995.

Sandoval, Ricardo. "Mexican Life at the Border: Why Are So
Many Teens Risking Their Lives to Cross the Border into the
United States?" *Junior Scholastic.* October 3, 2005, pp. 12–18.

Senker, Cath. *Immigrants and Refugees.* Milwaukee, WI: World
Almanac Library, 2005.

Williams, Mary E. *Opposing Viewpoints Series: Immigration.*
San Diego, CA: Greenhaven Press, 2004.

Zakaria, Fareed. "To Become an American." *Newsweek.* April 10,
2006, p. 39.

Index

Index

I

IIRA/IRA, 36
Immigration Act of 1965, 13, 15
Immigration Reform and Control
    Act of 1986, 39
Irish Potato Famine, 14

K

Know-Nothing Party, 14

L

Lazarus, Emma, 4–5, 51

M

Mariel Boatlift, 31
Medicaid, 24, 25
melting pot, concept of, 18
minimum wage, 20–21, 45, 47
Minuteman Project, 41

N

National Guard, 42
naturalization, 10, 27
"New Colossus," 4–5
New York Harbor, 4

P

pull factors, 8, 16, 37, 39, 40
push factors, 8, 12

Q

quotas, 12–13, 15, 20

R

Reagan, Ronald, 38
refugees, 26–27, 29, 30

S

salad bowl, concept of, 18
Schwarzenegger, Arnold, 41
Social Security, 9, 27, 28, 45, 48
Statue of Liberty, 4–6

U

U.S. Border Patrol, 41, 42, 46
U.S. embassy, 37

V

visas, 33, 45, 46

W

World War II (1939–1945), 38

About the Author

Renee Ambrosek is the author of several books for young adults, some of which are published using her married name, Renee Graves. She currently lives in Memphis with her husband, Alan, and her daughter, Gabriella, but she grew up in San Antonio, Texas, where many of her childhood friends were Hispanic. As a result, she has a particular interest in immigration issues, especially as they relate to children.

Photo Credits

Cover (left), pp. 39, 40 © David McNew/Getty Images; cover (right), p. 47 © Joe Raedle/Getty Images; p. 6 © Edwin Levick/Getty Images; p. 9 © AP/Wide World Photos; p. 11 © Lewis W. Hine/Museum of the City of New York/Getty Images; pp. 13, 25 © Tim Boyle/Getty Images; p. 17 © Underwood & Underwood/Corbis; p. 21 © Justin Sullivan/Getty Images; p. 23 © Mario Tama/AFP/Getty Images; pp. 27, 29 © Barry Williams/Getty Images; p. 32 © Bettmann/Corbis; p. 34 © Jewel Samad/AFP/Getty Images; p. 44 © Joyce Naltchayan/AFP/Getty Images; p. 50 © Ross D. Franklin/Getty Images.

Designer: Gene Mollica; **Editor:** Leigh Ann Cobb
Photo Researcher: Amy Feinberg